Charles C Capel

Trout Culture

A Practical Treatise on the Art of Spawning, Hatching and Rearing Trout

Charles C Capel

Trout Culture
A Practical Treatise on the Art of Spawning, Hatching and Rearing Trout

ISBN/EAN: 9783337139513

Printed in Europe, USA, Canada, Australia, Japan

Cover: Foto ©Andreas Hilbeck / pixelio.de

More available books at **www.hansebooks.com**

A PRACTICAL TREATISE

ON THE ART OF

SPAWNING, HATCHING, AND REARING TROUT.

BY

CHARLES C. CAPEL, F.R.M.S.

LONDON:

[ARDWICKE AND BOGUE, 192, PICCADILLY, W.

1877.

INTRODUCTION.

IN bringing out this little work on the Culture of Trout, the author feels that he is attempting to supply a great want, as many landed proprietors, desirous of stocking their waters with that fish, naturally wish for some simple practical work wherein they may find information which will serve for a help to the servant as well as to the master, especially in the absence of the latter.

The author, in his first attempt at Pisciculture, would have been truly thankful for such a guide ; and, with the hope that they may be of use to others, and enable them to enter upon a successful career, he now ventures to publish the results of his own practical experience.

His grateful acknowledgments are due to

the Rev. L. Stone for the account of the Russian or Dry method of Spawning, and for the Spawn and Hatching Tables, &c. ; also to Mr. Richard Edon, of the Museum of Fish Culture, South Kensington, London, for many valuable hints bearing on the subject.

All the methods of procedure recommended, have been personally tried, and nothing has been taken from the works of others, so far as the author is aware, without due acknowledgment.

CRAY FISHERY,
FOOTS CRAY, KENT.

CONTENTS.

CHAPTER VI.

CHAPTER VII.

CHAPTER VIII.

CHAPTER IX.

TROUT CULTURE.

CHAPTER I.

PRELIMINARY CONSIDERATIONS.

THE three qualities, most needed, in order to become a successful trout-rearer, are Patience, Endurance, and Ingenuity. Without these no enterprise can well succeed, and pisciculture is assuredly no exception. In fish breeding patience is required, because its duties are what some might call monotonous: the round of work is regular, and must be carried on much the same, day after day, month after month, with, it may be, very slight variation; but still, the work soon grows into a habit, and, when once a system has been formed, the tiresome-ness of daily duties is much lessened; and from daily observation a sort of attachment spontaneously grows up between the attendant and his charges, which does much to dispel the monotony of the work.

Endurance, again, is needed, as the spawning and hatching of trout take place in winter, and the coldness of the water is very trying to the hands and arms; this, however, is but a small matter, if the rest of the body be protected by good woollen clothing, and the feet encased in waterproof boots. The subject of clothing will, however, receive more attention at the end of this chapter.

Ingenuity, again, is essential, because accidents and misfortunes will happen even to the experienced, and then, he who is the most ready to devise a remedy, or means of escape, will find his quickness of resource amply repaid, and of the greatest value; as, if anything happens to young trout, unless speedily set right, it usually affects the whole of that 'stock. He, therefore, that would successfully rear trout must make up his mind to be constant to duty, fearless of difficulty and obstacle, and quick to act, ready to face cold, snow, and ice; he must be prepared also to buy experience at some cost; and it is the object of this little work to reduce that cost as much as possible.

We have put before the reader the unpleasant part of the picture; now, let us turn to the sunny side. What can be more enjoyable than a fine winter's morning, such as we often have in January, with the sunshine dancing among the ripples of the little streams, as they rattle over the golden gravel?

"Saw some fine fish up spawning in the Alders this morning, sir. Six or eight there, and lots in the stream above the farm." Cheering news, this, as we meet our faithful lieutenant outside the hatching-house, bustling about amongst nets, tins, &c. How one gloats over the prospect of a good day's spawning!

What a lot of intelligence the wily fishes evince, too, in doubling and baffling their pursuers! Personally, we would rather have a good day at this than at angling.

Again, what a charm there is in a well-ordered hatching-house, with its thousands and thousands of golden eggs covered with bloom like a ripe peach! Fish culture is indeed a charming amusement, free from cruelty, and full of enjoyment for anyone who has a love for Nature and her beauties.

Some one may, doubtless, think that the colouring of this picture has been laid on with a too generous hand : let him try for himself, and it is almost certain he will admit that there has been no exaggeration.

Some anglers celebrate the death of the first fish with " a glass round " ; we, on the other hand, inaugurate the existence of our first batch of eggs in the same way, wishing them health and long life.

Before this chapter closes, a few remarks on clothing may not be out of place, and, firstly, as to covering for the feet. From personal experience, we strongly prefer the thigh wading boots of indiarubber to the hide boots, as being much lighter, requiring no dressing, and if properly used, more comfortable. Two pairs are necessary, so as to permit the evaporation of the perspiration from the interior of one pair whilst the other is in use. Waterproof socks also tend very materially to preserve the boots, and, what is more, the health of the wearer, as they can easily be turned inside out and aired, thus keeping the foot of the boot dry and free from mouldiness.

One or two pairs of thick woollen socks should be worn under the rubber socks.

The body should be encased in woollen garments, upper and under, to resist the damp, as hatching-houses generally are, more or less, saturated with aqueous vapour. A pair of indiarubber gloves lined with wool will be found a most comfortable adjunct to the furniture of the fish-breeding establishment.

For the supply of waterproof articles we have long employed Mr. George Cording, of 125, Regent Street, and 199, Strand, and can speak very highly of his productions.

The first matter of a special nature, which it behoves us to consider, is of necessity the water in which we propose to grow trout. The phrase "to grow trout," may seem an odd expression ; but it is, nevertheless, perfectly correct. For, just as in good soil, well manured, and with favourable conditions of rainfall, &c., it is easy to grow good seed and secure a heavy crop, so in good water, with good. eggs, and a liberal supply of natural or artificial food, is it easy to rear or grow trout to an extent, both of number and size, which will fairly astonish those who are unacquainted with the mysteries of trout-life.

To hatch the eggs we only require pure

water, of which the hatching-house should have an ample supply. Whether this be derived from stream or spring, is of small consequence so long as the temperature be not liable to sudden changes, as these are likely to interfere with the gradual and even development of the embryo. On the whole, therefore, we are inclined to prefer spring water for our hatching operations. For rearing the fry when removed from the hatching boxes, we also require pure water, water that is free from pollutions. But it should be well stocked with insects and animalcules, as these afford a constant supply of natural food for the young fishes. It may be stream or spring water so long as these conditions are fulfilled, and the more nearly it approaches in its qualities to that in which the eggs were hatched, the nearer will it be to perfection as a receiving stream.

Any little stream, possessing these characters,

will answer for rearing purposes, and it should have a moderate current, not too strong for the very young fishes, but not still and lifeless —ripple and pool alternating form, perhaps, the best home for fry, as they can then select their own quarters. To be perfect in this respect it should vary in depth from a few inches to two feet, as this supplies all that is necessary for the growth of trout to any size.

Next in importance to the quality of the water is its quantity. This must be liberal and constant, as a stinted or unequal supply, especially at the hatching-house, is very injurious. Therefore, in planning an establishment this point should be kept well in view, so as to make sure that, under no circumstances, and by no accident, can the supply run short. To have to stint and starve the eggs, or to think of every pint of water that can be scraped and saved, adds greatly to the troubles of fish culture, and detracts very much from the results, as eggs hatched under unfavourable conditions will never thrive nor do well.

The means of supply, again, forms a matter of some importance. If the water be derived from waterworks, it will, of course, only be necessary to have it laid to the hatching-house, and to see that the pipes are sufficiently large. Hydraulic rams are expensive ; but if one be already on the estate, should it throw plenty of water, it may be used. However, there is always an uncertainty about rams, as the least thing puts them out of order, and it takes some time to induce the machine to work when once stopped. For instance, an eel gets under one of the valves in the night and stops the machine, and has to be removed by unseating the valve ; this empties the pipes, which then become charged with air, and it often takes some hours to force this out, and to obtain a fresh supply of water. A thaw after a sharp frost has almost always a very injurious effect on the action of hydraulic rams.

Where we can get satisfactory pumping power, by hand, horse, or steam, and a cistern of a sufficient size to hold twenty-four hours' supply for the whole hatching operations, we may be quite contented so far as water supply is concerned.

Lead piping may be used with perfect safety in fish culture, and junctions may also be made with indiarubber piping, a great convenience in altering or extemporizing apparatus.

CHAPTER II.

THE HATCHING-HOUSE.

HAVING treated of the water supply, we next pass on to the hatching-house, which may be of brick, wood, or stone. Any out-building may be turned to use if only it be well built, well lighted, and well floored. It should be roomy, as vast numbers of little odds and ends, such as nets, tin cans, &c., are wont gradually to accumulate. A neat dry locker or broad shelf is very handy for nets, and tin cans should be arranged in nests, one inside the other, if possible.

A small stove by which to warm the hands will be appreciated. The cistern or cisterns should, if practicable, be inside the house ; but on no account should these, or anything else, be.

C

allowed to obstruct the light. A dark hatching-house is a misery and an abomination. As to the size of the cistern or cisterns, that must be regulated by the magnitude of the contemplated operations; whatever this may be, their capacity should be ample. They may be made of wood, lined with zinc or lead, or of galvanized iron.

Having got the cistern fixed, the next thing is the filter; and, in spite of all that has been said in favour of flannel and sand as the medium, we ourselves have great faith in charcoal, and advise that the matter be entrusted to Mr. Fred Lipscombe, of 44, Queen Victoria Street, Mansion House, London.

In his hands we know we are safe, and if the filter be examined and cleansed by a competent person once or twice a year, a constant supply of pure water is ensured. A good, well-trapped drain must be constructed in such a position as may be best fitted to receive the waste water after it has done its work; and it will be a good plan to have the receiving surface of the drain below that of the floor, and to carry the waste pipes under the floor, thus hiding an unsightly object, and preventing any accidental trip of the foot when carrying eggs or fry. The planks covering the drain and waste pipes should be screwed to the joists, not nailed, so that if any obstruction occur they may at once be removed.

The lighting should be ample, either from skylights or side windows, as the construction of the building may require, and it is advisable to be able to cause a current of air to pass throughout the building when desired.

Odds and ends will accumulate, and shelves should be fitted up to receive them; and a strong bench well supported for pestle and mortar, meat slicer, &c., will be found useful. There should be a place for everything, and everything should be in its place. Something may be wanted in a hurry, and it should be at hand and in sight; there should be no rummaging and ransacking after it, as there is sure to be, if one thing be piled on another.

A "round" towel may be suspended near the little stove for drying the hands, and hand-bowls are useful for many purposes. A mop for the floor is always handy, as however carefully the work is carried on, water is sure to be spilled, and one is very liable to catch cold from standing on a damp floor.

If these cardinal points have been attended to, the intending breeder of fishes, whatever the size of his contemplated operations, may look around him with some satisfaction, as he may feel sure that however he may wish to alter the · smaller details of his establishment, the main plan need not be materially altered or disturbed.

CHAPTER III.

THE HATCHING APPARATUS.

IN this country troughs of wood, slate, or terra-cotta are almost universally in use for this purpose, and it must be confessed that for the amateur, at any rate, they are unquestionably the best and handiest form of apparatus. It may be very different in large establishments, where many hundreds of thousands of eggs are annually received ; but, as this little work is intended for the beginner and not for the professional pisciculturist, we omit all mention of the new American process and apparatus as foreign to the nature of the work, especially as they have not yet received a sufficient trial in this country.

Having thus determined on the employment of troughs, the next question is the material best fitted to our purpose. Terra-cotta, slate, and wood have been mentioned, but we feel disposed to select slate for the use of the amateur as being very clean, not so liable to break, chip, or crack as terra-cotta or earthenware, and not so likely to leak as wood. They are generally made about two feet ten inches long, six inches wide, with a depth of water of about three inches. They can be obtained ready fitted with spouts from the attendant or curator, Museum of Fish Culture, South Kensington ; or from Messrs. Beck and Beck, Beck's Wharf, Isleworth ; and these, where expense is no object, leave nothing to be desired. They are arranged in tiers one above the other, so that the spout of one will deliver to the next below it.

If, however, expense be a matter of consideration, wooden boxes may be used; but they must be very carefully made by a good carpenter, and very accurately fitted with tongue and groove joints ; these joints dressed with red-lead, nailed up tightly, and pitched inside and out; but even with all these precautions they often leak. Before being pitched, however, the spouts must be fitted ; these consist of pieces of ¾-inch lead pipe, about five inches long, tapered down at one end with a penknife, and slightly bent along their whole length. A hole is then bored with a stock and bit, the centre of which should be about three inches from the bottom of the inside of the box, and the pipe must be screwed and pressed into the hole until a small portion protrudes into the box ; this is to be flattened out around the edge of the hole so as to form a sort of rivet to hold the spout in position, and to prevent leakage. These boxes may obviously be made of any size—four and a half inches is a convenient height—and the length and breadth may be arranged to suit the requirements of the building. They are, however, so liable to leak, or what is technically called " sweat," that they are not recommended.

A good strong framework must be arranged
to support the troughs, of whatever material
they are constructed. It should resemble
a staircase, the steps being of the width of
the troughs, and arranged at such a height
relatively to one another that the spout of each
trough may properly deliver its water into that
below it.

When filling up an apparatus Mr. Edon sug-
gests that a lead pipe should be attached to the
water supply and carried along the whole length
of the back inner edge of each trough, being
twisted over the ends and so brought down to
the trough below. The other, or free end, is
squeezed together with pincers, and thus closed
water-tight. Small perforations are then made
with a fine pointed awl or other instrument, and
this gives a thorough aëration to the whole of
the water in each trough, and an equal supply
of fresh water throughout the apparatus. In
slate tanks or troughs the pipe may be fastened

to the back edge by straps of lead passed round the pipe and turned over the edge ; in wooden boxes by small tenter-hooks. This idea of Mr. Edon is truly valuable. It has been used at the writer's establishment, and found eminently useful. The spout of the bottom trough must be connected by indiarubber pipe, or otherwise, to a waste pipe leading to the drain, and of the same size as the spout.

In slate troughs, in order to confine the little fish after hatching, a light wooden frame, covered with fine perforated zinc, must be fitted just above the spout of the lowest trough, and also at any other point if desired, so as to separate the various species, if more than one is being hatched in the same apparatus. In wooden troughs the zinc or gauze may be carefully nailed directly on to the wood, after being pitched ; but must not be fastened flat on to the wood, but curved outwards a little so as not to cause too great a suction or draught of water, or else the fishes will be carried on to the stream and killed, and their bodies will block the screen and cause an overflow, thereby adding materially to the loss.

The zinc or gauze must be very fine, with holes no more than one-sixteenth or one thirty-second of an inch, as the fry have a tendency to work down stream, and will seek for any small aperture through which they can wriggle themselves, and will follow each other out in this manner if they can only find a crevice, to an extent which, however creditable to their ingenuity, is a sad loss to the breeder. Every care should therefore be taken to prevent this, and all should be made perfectly secure before the water is turned on.

High authorities state that fishes' eggs should be covered over and hatched in the dark. Light covers should therefore be provided, and they should have a hole or slot in them to permit the water to enter from the spout above.

The lids and lead pipes should have two

coats of a varnish, composed of two-thirds gas-tar and one-third turpentine, in order to prevent the oxidation of the lead, which is hurtful, and also to avoid the growth of slime or "fungus" on the wet surface of the wood.

The last point to be touched upon is the gravel.

This should be small—about the size of split peas. It may often be found lying loose on garden walks, and ought to be collected in dry weather; well washed, till the washing water runs off clear; and then boiled in a saucepan or copper, in order to destroy any germs of life which may remain in it. When cool it should be washed once more in filtered water, and it is then fit for use. A few days before eggs are expected, a thin layer is spread over the bottom of the trough, just enough to prevent its being seen, not more. The water may then be turned on a little to season the apparatus, which will then be ready for use.

In addition to his other apparatus the fish-
breeder will require a few (one or two) glass
tubes for moving and examining eggs and fry.
No description need be given of them, as the
curator of the Museum of Fish Culture at South
, Kensington always has a stock for sale. They
are used as follows : The tube is lightly held
by the third and fourth fingers of the right
hand, in such a manner that the thumb can
easily close the end ; the thumb being pressed
on the end, the bent part is thrust gently into
the water towards the eggs or fry to be lifted.
The thumb is then suddenly removed from the
end of the tube for a moment, when the water
and eggs, &c., will rush up. The thumb is again
applied, and the other end of the tube raised by
· a circular motion of the wrist, when its contents
may be examined, and, on removing the thumb,
may be returned to the trough or any other
vessel. A few trials give dexterity in the use of
this serviceable little piece of apparatus. A few

feathers stripped to within an inch of the end, and used for moving eggs under water, are also of service. A pair of spring forceps or nippers will also be required for picking out dead eggs, &c. They should be about six or seven inches long, and have rounded points : they may be obtained at the surgical instrument makers' shops.

The above is all that will be required for those who buy eggs and hatch them out. Those who spawn their own fishes will require small flue or trammel nets of a suitable size to stretch across the little spawning streams up which the trout run to spawn. They will also need one or two landing nets fixed on to iron frames, fitted with light poles for handles. The writer uses frames two feet wide by one foot in depth, the bottom of the frame, or the side opposite the handle, being square, so as to scoop well under a fish ; and by this means a pair of fish may be frequently caught, as they are too intent on

their own affairs to notice anything else. The
irons or frames are punched with holes at intervals of about an inch, by which the net is
attached to them with iron or copper wire.

Two or three tin or galvanized iron foot-pans,
to hold the fish when caught, and two or three
Yorkshire pudding dishes, to act as spawning
tins or pans, will also be required; together
with a light can to hold the washed eggs, and a
mug to wash them with.

Whilst mentioning the spawning apparatus,
it will not be out of place to refer to the boxes
in which fry may be kept, and which are very
convenient at spawning time, when the fry (or
yearlings rather) have been turned out into
the open streams; they are handy recipients
for unripe fish, and those which are ripe, but
which it is not convenient to spawn at the
moment. Their size may be made to suit the
little streams, and the length may vary from
twelve to twenty feet, as the fancy and re-

quirements of the owner may direct. They should have lids of open skeleton framework, carefully covered with fine wire netting to keep out the kingfishers, for these pests clear out boxes at a marvellous rate if once they get to know their way into them. The writer speaks from bitter experience on this point, and can personally vouch for the insidious character of this the most beautiful of British birds. The ends of the boxes should have frames sliding in grooves, on which perforated zinc can be fastened; the size of the perforations in this will vary, of course, with that of the fish: fry, at first, one-sixteenth of an inch; after they have grown somewhat, one-eighth; and for spawning fish, three-sixteenths or one-fourth of an inch. In some waters zinc, especially if perforated, is so powerfully acted upon that in six months it crumbles away. In these iron may be used, as water that corrodes zinc has no action on iron.

Perforated iron is of course more expensive, but in such cases we have no alternative, except that of constantly renewing the zinc, which would soon outrun the prime cost of the iron.

CHAPTER IV.

SPAWNING.

·WHEN cold weather fairly sets in, sooner or later, according to river and season, the trout run up into the small side streams, where shallow, rippling water and bright gravel are to be found. Sometimes they come up together in pairs, sometimes singly. In some years the spawning season lasts only a fortnight ; in others, as last year, for eight or ten weeks. This mainly depends on the weather and the state of the main stream. Before the fish come up, the mud should be cleared away, overgrown weeds cleared out, and the gravel raked over, so as to be inviting to them. Shelter of some sort should be given to induce the fish to stop near the beds. Broken or old drain pipes may be provided, and boards may be moored in the stream for them to lie under.

When " up " on the beds, which may be seen at a glance, as the cock trout, or milter, works the gravel into heaps, the nets must be got out and the fish caught.   One of the little flue or trammel nets should be set at each end of the beds, and then the shelters or covers of the beds may be cautiously removed, when the fish will fly into the nets.   By the deft use of the large landing nets, pairs of fish may be caught as they lie in the stream ; but it is always advisable to have the trammels set, as then there is no risk of escape.

If there are any holes under the banks made by water-rats they should be examined, as trout frequent them.   If the net will not reach right to the end of the hole, the arm must be thrust in, and the hand will often find a fish at the end of the opening: the hand is passed gently along so as to be able to grasp the fish just above the tail, it is then suddenly closed, and the fish "tailed out" on to the bank, and put into a tub or foot-pan of water whilst others are sought for.

When all have been caught, the sexes should be determined, and the unripe fish, if any, transferred to the box mentioned at the end of the previous chapter.

The sexes are readily distinguished, as at spawning time the eggs will be felt in the spawner or hen fish, whilst in the male the milt being a liquid, is easily recognized. In taking a fish out of a net, if in anything like proper order for spawning, a few eggs or a drop of milt will generally appear, even with the gentlest handling. Unless a fish is thoroughly ripe it should be kept in the box till it is so, as unripe eggs or milt are quite useless for hatching purposes.

When the sexes are determined, and the ripe fish separated, we have to consider the proportionate numbers of each sex. Some days we have more cocks than hens, others the reverse, or even all hens and no cocks. As one cock will, if "full," suffice to impregnate two, or even three, hens, it is advisable if possible to reserve a cock in case of being short of milt on a future occasion.

Having mentioned all this, we will suppose that proper arrangements have been made, and that the actual process of spawning is being carried out. The spawning tin or pan is either laid on the ground or on a box, tilted a little to one end by a stone or stick, *quite dry*. A hen fish is taken out of the tub and allowed to kick about for a few seconds ͵to render it less difficult to hold, and induce it to yield its eggs more freely. The spawner then, with a piece of flannel, holds the head͵ of the fish carefully, but firmly, in his left hand, and his assistant keeps it extended by grasping it just above the tail, but below the vent, a piece of flannel being used to secure a firm grasp. The fish is held sideways, with the vent as near the bottom of the spawning pan as possible, and the spawner with his right hand strips the fish. Some operators begin at the upper end of the ovary, which extends nearly to the pectoral fin, and carry the pressure gently, but quickly, to the vent, only using the thumb and fourth finger. Others first press out the eggs nearest the vent, and then work up the ovary, squeezing the eggs out portion by portion until all are removed. So long as no backward pressure is allowed, which would injure the fish, this is a good method.

Whatever plan be adopted, it must be carried out rapidly and gently : if the fish be faint, or refuses to yield all its eggs, it must be put into a vessel of fresh water for a few minutes, whilst another hen is stripped, by which time it will probably have recovered, and can be completely emptied. When one or two hens have been stripped, the cock is held over the eggs, and his milt taken in the same way, except that the testes or milt bags do not extend so far up the fish as ovaries ; in fact, not much more than half-way between the vent and pectoral fins. When spawned, each fish should be carefully returned to the water, and, if faint, supported between two stones, head up stream, until able to look after itself. When the milt has been taken, the pan should be tilted a little so as to mix the milt with the eggs, and then left a minute or two ; after which a little water must be added, enough to cover the eggs, and the pan set aside until the eggs (which at first cohere very strongly) have completely separated. They may then be washed with clean water, once or twice changed, and be transferred to the egg can. This should be filled with water, and the eggs poured into it from an angle of the spawning pan. They at once sink to the bottom, and the superfluous water runs over the side. The separation of the eggs takes from ten to twenty minutes, and this interval may be used in spawning other trout, if at hand.

Some operators spawn all their fish in one pan, but we think the course above suggested preferable for many reasons. The eggs of two hens are, in our opinion, enough to have in one pan ; but, if short of milt, of course if there are three, or even four hens to one cock, all must be spawned in one pan.

We should advise anyone intending to spawn fish to have a look at the casts in the Museum of Fish Culture, South Kensington. He will there see exactly how the organs of generation are placed in the salmonidæ, and will gain a good deal of useful information on that and other points by his visit.

By the old, or wet method, now almost, if not quite, obsolete, the fish and the hands of the operator were plunged in a vessel of water, the eggs taken were very carefully washed, and then the milt was stripped into a separate vessel of

water and mixed with the eggs. A hatch of
sixty per cent. was thought very good in those
days, and so undoubtedly it was, if the result be
regarded by the light of our modern knowledge.
The thing would seem to be almost impossible,
but for one fact lately made public by Mr.
Jackson, of the Southport Aquarium, whose
microscopic investigations of the movements of
milt in water are very important. He tells us
that when milt finds itself in water the spermatozoa distribute themselves throughout it, each
keeping an equal distance from the other, so as
to miss nothing. In fact, he compares the
appearance of these objects, seen in the field of
a microscope, with the patterns of shot, as ad-
vertised by makers of close-shooting guns ; but
points out that the regularity of the distance of
the spermatozoa from each other was almost, if
not quite, invariably observed, each one main-
taining its position relatively to the rest, as the
milt spread through the water. This is a matter

of the greatest importance, and should receive further attention, as it leads us to a clearer comprehension of the manner in which eggs are naturally fertilized in a stream, and cannot fail to be of great interest to the student of physiology.

We have said that under the old régime sixty per cent. was thought good. By degrees, however, less water was employed, and the result. was found to justify the innovation ; so that, gradually one vessel was substituted for two, and very little water was used. The veteran pioneer in pisciculture, Seth Green, found this out many years ago, as Mr. Stone tells us in 'Domesticated Trout'; and, though ready to impart any other fact to others, he carefully kept this to himself, saying that it was as good as a patent to him, and so it was. However, before the advent of the Russian method, men on this side of the Atlantic had come to the same conclusion, and eighty per cent. of impregnation had been reached; aye, ninety also, but only by old and knowing operators. By the new process the mere tyro may obtain ninety or ninety-five per cent.

The following account showing the discovery and superiority of the " Russian " or dry method of spawning was printed in the ' New York Citizen and Round Table,' May 27, 1871, and published in ' Domesticated Trout,' by L. Stone:

" In his experiments, M. Vrasski had followed the counsels given in French and German works on pisciculture, but the results obtained were far from being brilliant. In reality, at each hatching, he obtained but an insignificant number. ' From many thousands of eggs,' says he in a letter, 'there were only some dozens of young fry. The rest of the eggs were lost and spoilt for want of being impregnated. I have, however, followed with scrupulous exactness all the directions given in the manuals for fecundation.' In the autumn of

1856, M. Vrasski was occupied with the microscopic examination of the eggs and milt, and kept a journal in which he registered the least circumstances and incidents relative to each fecundation that he effected. Two months of persistent efforts brought the desired results. The journal and the microscope proved to him that the cause of his failure proceeded precisely from the exact observation of all the counsels of the foreign manuals. It is necessary for fecundation that the spermatozoa of the milt of the male should penetrate the eggs of the female. In order to do this, the manuals recommended receiving the eggs in a vessel of water; afterwards, to receive in another vessel of water the milt of the male; and, lastly, to turn the diluted milt on to the eggs. By his journal, kept with scrupulous exactness, M. Vrasski convinced himself that the fecundation was so much the less complete, according as the mixture of the milt and eggs had been the most delayed. If ten minutes elapsed between obtaining the milt and the mixing of it with the eggs, the fecundation failed almost entirely. His observations, and the microscopic researches of the eggs and milt, showed that;

"First. When received in water at the moment of issuing from the fish, the eggs absorb the water, and preserve the power of being impregnated only as long as this absorption is not finished : that is to say, during a half hour at the utmost. Once saturated with water, the eggs do not absorb any spermatozoa : but if received into dry vessels on issuing from the fish, the eggs remain, on the contrary, in a neutral state for a lengthened time, and do not lose the power, when placed in water, of receiving the spermatozoa.

"Second. The spermatozoa of the milt, in falling into the water, commence immediately, with much vigour and rapidity, to make movements, which only last, however, for a minute and a half, or two at the most; when this time is elapsed, only in some few spermatozoa can there be seen particular movements and agonized convulsions.

"When, at the issuing from the fish, the milt is received in a dry vessel, it does not change for many hours, and during this interval the spermatozoa do not use the power of beginning to move as they do when placed in contact with water. Closed in a dry vial, and well corked, the milt preserves its impregnating virtue during six days.

"From these observations, as also from the fact that the eggs as well as the milt are obtained slowly, their entire mass not being able to issue at once, M. Vrasski arrived at the conclusion, that when they were received in water, the greater part of the eggs attempted to saturate themselves with it, and the spermatozoa ceased to move almost before it was possible for the fish-breeder to mix the eggs with the diluted milt. M. Vrasski then adopted the system of dry vessels, and turned the milt on the eggs directly he put them in water. The success was complete : all the eggs were impregnated without one exception."

The above speaks for itself, so that all we need further do is to congratulate M. Vrasski on his success, and thank Mr. George Shephard Page for publishing them in America, whence we have received them through the Rev. L. Stone, an eminent American pisciculturist.

To revert to the eggs which we left in the egg can. This must be carried home carefully, and its contents distributed in the troughs by the aid of the glass tube ; the covers are then to be placed on the troughs, and a good supply of water turned on. In arranging eggs in troughs it is always advisable to fill from the lowest upwards, as by this means the shells of the first hatched lot do not interfere with those eggs which hatch later on.

As to the number of eggs to be allowed to a square foot of trough, to secure perfect health and strength, we should recommend that the number should be restricted to a thousand, which is a perfectly safe number; and is, after all, amply sufficient for the private hatching-house, in which quality, not quantity, is the great object in view.

In arranging eggs a feather may be of great service, if lightly used ; as, by its means, the eggs may be easily separated, so that no two may touch each other. They will hatch out better for this, as each egg will have a current of oxygen-bearing water passing all round it, which cannot be the case when all the eggs are left in heaps.

The operator should be very careful to see that the eggs are well and carefully cleansed before distributing them in the troughs, as the object in view is to have eggs, gravel, and water in the apparatus, *and nothing else.*

Eggs are a favourite prey of a number, of enemies. Some fish prefer them to any other sort of food, and rats or mice will eat them greedily if they get a chance. Care should therefore be taken to keep the troughs closely covered if peril be apprehended from the latter source.

CHAPTER V.

HATCHING.

IF everything were quite right, hatching would be a very easy affair. If every egg were impregnated, and no enemies existed, the fish-hatcher's labours would be light indeed ; but this is not always the case, especially at first. If, however, the directions about the spawning be faithfully carried out, and the hatching apparatus fitted as above advised, we may safely anticipate good results.

When the eggs are once placed in the hatching troughs, they must remain there until hatched, or at any rate until the eyes of the embryo are distinctly visible through the shell. When thus " eyed " they may be moved carefully, if needful, and even packed in moss and sent long dis-

E

tances ; but, excepting when sending a present
of eggs to a friend, there will never be any
necessity for doing so in the private hatching-
house, and the eggs should be left at rest until
hatched out.

They must, however, be daily examined, and
all dead eggs carefully removed with the forceps
or nippers ; and great care must be taken at
first in doing this so as not to injure a living
one near it, and hence the benefit of spread-
ing the eggs at first, and once for all, with a
feather or otherwise, when laying them in the
trough.

If kept in heaps the feather is used to spread
them, and thus the odds are that a second one
is formed, and the daily examination is much
prolonged, to say nothing of the bother of
always having a feather in hand when examining the eggs.

The tyro will naturally ask, "How am I to
tell a dead from a living egg ?" Let him have

no anxiety about that, as a dead egg can be told in a second, even by an inexperienced eye. A good living egg is translucent, and has a beautiful bloom on it like that of a ripe Muscat grape; a dead egg is opaque and white, and when once seen can never be mistaken.

These dead eggs should be picked out carefully every day, as, if left in the water, a species of alga grows upon them, and spreads over the living eggs in their vicinity, and by killing them would, if left alone, in time do incalculable mischief.

Every care, therefore, should be taken to secure a perfect impregnation, as the more successful it is, the less labour will there be in removing blind eggs; and this labour is of no pleasant kind, as the work has to be done with the hands, dabbling in the water very often with the air below the freezing point, and the running water very little above it.

If, however, ripe milt and eggs have been

used, and all has been done well, the labours
of the day will be very light, and the sense of
success will buoy up the heart under any little
hardship or difficulty.

It has been said before that the eggs when
once placed in the box or trough must remain
undisturbed until fully eyed, if not hatched.
Too much stress cannot be laid on this point, as,
if moved before they have eyed out, fully one-
half of the eggs are sure to die. It seems
strange that what kills one egg will not destroy
another; it may, however, we think be at-
tributed to the greater natural vitality of some
eggs than of others. Some will, perhaps, at-
tribute it to a faulty impregnation; but we
think, under the dry system this can hardly be
the case. Whatever the theory used to account
for it, the fact remains; and all care and pre-
vision should be taken to prevent a necessity
arising for taking so perilous a step.

If the eggs appear to be dirty, or covered

with a fine dust or sediment, a watering pot, with a rose bearing very small perforations, should be employed to wash it off; but if the filter be Lipscombe's, and the covers kept closely on, there will be little chance of this occurring ; however, should there be the slightest appearance of it when the eggs are examined in the glass tube, the remedy should be promptly administered, as sediment is a very dangerous thing, for it chokes the eggs by preventing the free absorption of oxygen from the water, on which the health and development of the embryo so much depend. Dirty eggs may hatch, but will never thrive.

Should the purchase of " eyed ova " be made, any fresh variety be introduced, or a greater stock be required than the river itself will supply, they will generally be received packed in round tin boxes, either loose, in wet moss, or enclosed in folds of muslin or mosquito netting, with layers of wet moss above and below them.

The tin has holes in the bottom, and must be put into a vessel rather deeper than itself, and water must be added ; when, on removing the lid and top layer of moss, the water will work up through the holes in the bottom and cover the eggs. If these be loose, as much as possible of the moss and *all* the heavy parts of it having been removed, the whole arrangement is to be carried under a tap and a gentle stream of water directed to one side of the vessel ; this will drive over the moss, with the assistance perhaps of a feather, and the eggs will settle in a state of purity ; they may then be quickly transferred to a trough, or be washed further in any other vessel, as may be convenient.

When muslin is used, the moss is cleared away till the muslin appears, and all moss adhering to it is removed ; then the edges are folded together, and the whole lifted out and shaken, and gently separated in a vessel of pure water ; the eggs sink, and any floating moss may be driven over as before, after all the layers of eggs have been shaken out in the water.

In sending eggs away the reverse operation is performed. The tin is sunk in a vessel of water, then a layer of soft, well-washed *Sphagnum* moss is put on the bottom, then one fold of muslin, then the eggs are carefully distributed over this with a glass tube, and arranged with a feather or thin glass rod, so that no two eggs are in contact, then a second fold of muslin, and the operation repeated as before till completed. Next, a good thick layer of moss is put on and the box drained; then, should the moss have sunk down, it is topped up with a fresh layer to completely fill the box, and the lid is put on. Finally the tin is packed firmly in sawdust, in a wooden box, the lid screwed down, and sent off..

In estimating the number of eggs in a fish, the rule is that one thousand eggs go to a pound of weight. Thus a half-pound fish will have five hundred ; a pounder, one thousand ; a two pounder, two thousand, and so on.

American trout eggs take very nearly, if not quite, the same time, under similar conditions, to hatch out as those of this country. Mr. Seth Green, no mean authority, says that in water at 50° Fahr., the eggs will hatch in fifty days, and every degree warmer or colder makes five days difference, the eggs hatching earlier in warmer, and being retarded in their development in colder water. Mr. Green also says that if the eggs hatch in fifty days, the yolk sac lasts thirty ; if hatched in seventy days, the sac remains forty-five. We are indebted to Mr. Stone for this information, which will be found generally reliable, though subject to alteration or modification by circumstances.

Seasons vary, and times of spawning vary (though within comparatively narrow limits), consequently no hard and fast rule as to time of incubation can be laid down. Late eggs may very likely hatch in a far shorter time than early ones, as the water at the end of February, and in March and April, will be warming up, and consequently the development of the embryo will be more rapid.

No one, however, should be anxious to see the eggs hatch out quickly; the more slowly they hatch the better, healthier, and stronger will the fish be. · If the eggs have "eyed" out strongly, and the form of the fish be dark and lusty in the egg, let no one have any anxiety about earliness of breaking the shell.

Some day or other a little dark-looking thing will be seen in one or other of the troughs, and an attempt be made to remove it with the nippers, when the little object will wriggle away and seek protection amongst the eggs. These at this period appear much swollen, and of a tint and with a bloom like a ripe peach. On examining the little stranger in the glass tube, it will appear as a mere threadlike body, with two very prominent eyes, resting on a round yellow ball of oil. On using a lens it will be seen that the blood-vessels are spread out into and over this vesicle of oil or yolk, whence the necessary food is obtained in this, which is called the "Alevin" stage of a trout's existence.

Nature thus caters for the young fish for from a month to seven or eight weeks, according to temperature; heat accelerating and cold retarding the consumption of the oil in the vesicle and the development of the body. Having all its needs supplied, it rests pretty quietly for a day or two, and only wriggles at intervals; but about the fifth day from the general hatching out of that batch of eggs, a general desire to hide becomes manifest. Accordingly in every angle of the trough, except where the water is disturbed by the stream falling in from the trough above, there will be

seen a writhing, wriggling mass of alevins, each
trying with might and main to hide itself under
its neighbours, all heads directed towards the
corner, and the strongest youngsters lying in,
until forced out by superior numbers ; and this
goes on for some time, it may be a fortnight or
three weeks, according to the temperature of
the water. During this time the alevins will
have gained greatly in size, grace, and sym-
metry. They will have become wonderfully
active, swimming rapidly up and down the
tube, and their fins will be seen to have grown,
and the tail developed to a surprising extent.
The umbilical sac or vesicle, too, will have half,
or more than half disappeared, having been
gradually absorbed during this period, to yield
the necessary nourishment for the evolution of
the various organs of the fish, which were at
first in a rudimentary state.

After this they gradually separate, leaving
the corners of the trough and covering its whole

length at pretty even distances, having the appearance, at a distance, of extra thick black pins. They do not move much now ; however, on looking over them a few will be seen in motion at intervals ; but it can scarcely be realized that these seemingly impotent creatures will, in a week or two, be in incessant motion ; yet such is the case, as the rest appears to be needed for the complete development of the swimming apparatus ; when this is duly furnished, they will be seen to rise spontaneously in the water, and stem the stream flowing over them ; though they still carry a vestige of the umbilical vesicle or sac.

There is hardly a more enjoyable sight in store for the breeder of trout than to see a trough full of young trout balancing themselves in the water, with every fin in action, now stemming the stream as it runs in from above, and then retiring to a quieter place to recover themselves after the exertion.

Now and for some time after, a great tendency will be manifested by the young fish to
go down stream, especially at night. The writer
has almost emptied the bottom trough of a
series, and next morning has found it crowded
with others. Every effort and much ingenuity
will be evinced by the fish ; therefore the
greatest care should be taken to see that no
chance fault or flaw is left uncared for in the
outlet screen, or great will be the loss, as the
trout will follow each other like a flock of
sheep, if once an opening be discovered. This
is a very pleasant time for the fish-breeder ;
the fish require no food as yet, and very few
die ; so that he has only to look over his stock
every day, to pick out any chance dead ones
carefully, and to admire the wealth of life
moving beneath his eyes. .

Before closing this chapter, to treat of the
method of feeding and rearing the completely
formed fish, we think it advisable to repeat two

or three of the chief points in hatching, on which success depends.

Have everything in perfect order before commencing operations, and the water running gently through the apparatus a day or two before eggs are expected. Use only freely flowing eggs and milt, use a sufficiency of the latter, leave eggs and milt together for a minute or two, and, on adding water, let the eggs separate perfectly before cleansing.

On no account move eggs about till well " eyed," and pick out dead ones daily.

CHAPTER VI.

REARING.

WHEN the umbilical sac or vesicle has quite disappeared, and the young fry can swim actively about, the time will have come for feeding to commence.

No one need have any anxiety as to how soon to offer food, as the fry will plainly show when they are inclined for it, by darting at any little insect or other small object floating on the water. Throw a few gnats on the water, if there be any uncertainty, or cast in a very few small blood-worms, and, if ready for their meal, the fry will cause a total disappearance of gnat or worm in a marvellously short time.

It is wise at this 'time daily to test the most forward lot in this manner, as some of the fry are sure to be more forward than others and require food sooner. Whenever a lot of fish show themselves ready to feed they must have a regular supply of it daily at proper intervals.

The most "growing" food for trout is insects, as proved by experiments of Mr. Stoddart, who confined three lots of fish in three tanks, feeding one lot on worms, another on live minnows, and the third on insects: those fed on insects outweighed the other two lots put together.

Where gnats are to be found in large swarms, and when there, is plenty of leisure to secure a supply with an insect net, they form a first-rate food, as the fry are very fond of them, grow very rapidly on them, and get into the habit of "rising to the fly," which is a great advantage to them in after life, when turned loose to shift for themselves.

Unless, however, the supply is perfectly ample, the fish-rearer had better look elsewhere for his commissariat, and reserve the gnats, &c., for a relish, as whatever else may form the staple of the diet, they are always a very welcome addition. In catching gnats a common gauze entomologist's net is used, and when caught they may be killed by confining them in the end of the net with one hand and striking it with the other.

Failing gnats, blood-worms are the best and most nourishing food. They are obtained from the mud of the Thames, and doubtless might be found elsewhere. They may be procured from the curator, Museum of Fish Culture, South Kensington, and elsewhere; but the writer can only say that those he has obtained at the museum are the best. They must be kept in a good sized vessel, so that they can spread out, and must have running water, or they soon die, and yield by their decomposition a most painful odour, sickening in the extreme. As long as they are healthy they will clump up together, and present a beautiful appearance. A portion of the clump is to be torn off and given to the fish, care being taken, especially at first, to spread them about in the water, so that the fry can get at them easily, and share alike.

Three or four meals a day are quite enough at first, and the worms or gnats (or both) should be continued for six or eight weeks, till the fry have grown plump and strong and are able to take larger food.

But before this the thinning-out process must be taken in hand. Trout require plenty of elbow room, and if they are cooped up too closely will not thrive or feed so well, and very often take to nibbling at each other, or worse, to habits of utter cannibalism, things to be avoided by all means; therefore the fish-rearer should, ere this, have made arrangements for the transfer of his fry to quarters where more space will be afforded to them.

There are three ways of doing this, either by

building tanks, or by keeping them in boxes in running streams, or by turning the fry into the open stream, and confining them within safe limits by screens at each end.

Where a comparatively small number of fry have to be dealt with, or only a few are kept for show, the tank system proves very useful. It merely consists in building large tanks of wood, glass, or slate, in or near the hatching-house, or in some convenient spot, placing a perforated screen over the outlets, and running over the fry a good supply of unfiltered water ; the more this is charged with animal life the better, as the young trout will thus find a constant suitable stream of food flowing over them, amidst which they will have a good selection of varied diet of the best and most natural form. In addition to this, however, they should have regular meals of artificial food ; but of this more anon.

Boxes in streams, with screens of zinc or iron

at each end, have many advantages, especially where the open stream itself would be objectionable or unsuitable, either from the presence of too many natural enemies, or from other causes. Reference was made to this matter at the end of Chapter III., so that only a few hints on construction need be given here. The best way to set to work, in the writer's opinion, is to determine the length of the box, or boxes, by that of the longest planks to be obtained in the vicinity, as the expense involved in an extra length of a few feet is the merest trifle, whereas the benefit derived from the extra space thereby obtained is very great. Supposing the water be a foot deep, and the box four feet wide, every extra foot of length gives the fry four cubic feet more swimming space, or twenty-five gallons more water to spread about in.

The length and width determined, the construction is so easy that any man about the estate who has the most elementary notions of

carpentry can put it together. It should be
built, we think, on the edge of the stream if
practicable, so as to be rolled into position in
the water with as little difficulty as possible.
The sides are first formed by laying the three
planks forming a side on two pieces of stout
"quartering," each piece 27 inches long, placed
two and a half inches from the squared ends of
the planks (which have been previously cut to
the same length), and nailing or screwing firmly
together. Cross-pieces or braces should then be
nailed across the side so as to strengthen them
and prevent "winding"; and these should be
opposite each other on the two sides. The width
being determined, say three or four feet, the end
boards are cut, and nailed to the outer edge of
the "quartering" of each side, so as to unite the
sides, which must of course be parallel, and the
ends square and true. The boards forming the
bottom are now cut to the right length to
stretch over from one side to the other, and

nailed or screwed firmly on, care being taken to avoid leaving any aperture by which the fry can escape. If the box seems to want " stiffness," cross-pieces may be let in with a slight dovetail where the braces are fixed to the sides on the top, and this will make it a strong, sound job.

The ends should be fitted with grooved or " rabbeted " slides, and frames, covered with perforated zinc or iron, closely fitted, work in these, a large aperture having been cut in the end board at the bottom, or the bottom plank of each end may be entirely removed, a slip being nailed on to the " quartering " to afford a firm even bed for the slide and frame.

The skeleton lid should be formed in lengths, so as not to be unwieldy, and be covered with inch mesh wire netting to exclude enemies. It may, if desired, be fitted with hasps, staples, and padlocks. Before use, and whilst dry, it should be dressed inside with two coats, outside with one coat, of a mixture of two-thirds gas-tar and one-third turpentine. When dry, it may be rolled over on its side, with the bottom nearest the stream. Plenty of strength should be at hand to help this box or "ark" to the spot assigned for its resting place, for it must be brought right to the edge of the stream, with the bottom of the box slightly overhanging ; on raising it to an angle of about forty-five degrees the weight will cause it to slide gracefully into the water. It must next be adjusted in its proper place, and be held down till the water has filled it, when, after a little pressure from above has been brought to bear on it, a slight "bedding" of the bottom takes place, and it is fit, in twenty-four hours, for the reception of the fish, which may then be removed from the troughs and taken across in pails or other vessels to the stream.

If, however, the stream is in every way suitable, and the natural enemies of the fry not in greater abundance than can be thoroughly checked, the best and most natural way of rearing is to confine them in a portion of the open stream, say about 100 or 150 yards long, by wire or zinc screens fixed at each end; there they can range about, gather much food, from amongst the water plants, and from the grasses and shrubs overhanging the water. They must, however, have plenty of shelters into which they can retreat when danger of any sort threatens : these should consist of drain pipes, half-round tiles, bits of slate supported on stones, and great "burrs" from a brick-field, these last, especially in the case of older fish, all impede the operations of poachers, and afford, also, a welcome shade from the heat of a summer sun.

Before, however, an open stream is used for fry, all the weeds and mud should be re-moved, and the height of the water carefully noted, as weeds have a great tendency to heap the water up and give it an artificial height,

which is immensely above the natural level
when cleared out effectually. The writer, at the
moment of writing this, has but just returned
from visiting a stream of this sort, which, instead
of holding a foot or more of water, has not more
than three inches of depth, and in a dry season
would require to be dammed up by artificial
means.

If a few little falls can, under any circumstances, be made in the stream, they will be
advantageous to the fry, as they like strong
rippling water; these falls also tend to oxidize
the water, by exposing it in thin films to the air,
and have a neutralizing effect on any impurity
that may, by any chance, find its way in.
Water plants have this effect also, and should,
therefore, be encouraged to a moderate extent,
especially as they also act as shelters or hides.

The woodwork required for the screens at
each end of the water consists of a " sole-plate,"
a good solid slab of timber some six feet longer

than the width of the stream, having two strong uprights mortised into it about three feet from each end, and carrying grooves to receive the slide on which the zinc or iron screen is fastened. These uprights are braced to the ends of the sole-plate by "struts" or buttresses, with planking nailed to them so as to form "wings," which extend into the bank and prevent the water working round instead of going through the perforations of the screen, a thing which, in their absence, it is sure to do. A firm bottom is selected, and branches are made on each side of the bank to bed the wings on. The bottom is levelled, and the sole-plate is bedded carefully on it; and the stones and earth are rammed well in round the wings.

Large stones and bricks should be well worked up to the sole-plate on both sides, and for some distance, and should be well dressed with puddled clay; this in its turn being covered with gravel and fine shingle, as we have two difficulties to contend with. On the upper side we have the head of water, which, even if only of a few inches in height, will assuredly, unless well checked as above advised, work its way under the sole-plate and well up on the other side, thus affording a free egress to the fry, which, always on the look-out for an outlet, will not be slow to take advantage of it.

On the under side we have fish that are always alive to the advantages of a good shelter, with a flow of water through it. They therefore will work most assiduously to dig a hole under the screen and hide there. These things must be carefully attended to, or the loss of many fish is a certainty.

Having the place in order, whether tank, box, or stream, the next thing is to catch the fry out of the troughs, and, as they are by this time wonderfully active, the glass tube is no longer of any use, and is, accordingly, superseded by a light hand-net. The frame of this, made of wire, is of such a size as just to work easily inside the troughs, and is fixed into a short wooden handle; it is covered with muslin, and used with the right hand, a bowl or other vessel being held in the left so as to be ready to receive the fry when caught. At first the unsuspecting little creatures will be very easily swept up, but gradually the last few become very cunning by experience, and dodge the net with wonderful speed and dexterity. It is sometimes a good plan to use a syphon of indiarubber tubing and draw off the water into one of the lower tanks. Almost every one of the fry will make for the exit as the water sinks, and the few remaining may easily be got out by tilting the trough and sweeping them up in the net as the water flows back when the trough is again lowered.

Having caught the fry they must be taken in pails, or other vessels, to their new residence, and there set free, by gently turning the pail over when in the water. They will swim away, and endeavour to hide themselves, making free use of the artificial shelters provided for them.

Having treated of the food suited for the fry for the first six weeks after feeding, and of their removal before or at that time to the place where the next year's, or two years', growth will take place, we may return to the subject of feeding.

After supplying the fry with blood-worms or gnats for six or eight weeks, according to their strength, a change of food should be made; but it must not take place until they fly well at the food and eat it up before it reaches the bottom. They may leave the gnats uneaten without harm, as these insects float on the surface and do no damage beyond choking up a few of the holes in the screens. Unconsumed blood-worms, too, are perfectly innocuous, as they live in water, and will tend to purify the water by removing organic matter; but the foods to be hereafter mentioned, if left uneaten, will sink to the bottom, and there decomposing give rise to death and decimation.

Raw meat, especially beef, chopped fine, is a very good, nourishing diet, much to be recommended. It is easily prepared by one of the numerous machines sold for such purposes; " Starret's Patent American Meat Chopper " answers well for this, and may be obtained at the establishment of Mr. E. Cox, 117, High Holborn, London, for the sum of thirty shillings.

Raw meat pounded with arrowroot biscuit is also very useful, and in the writer's opinion, leaves little to be desired. It is thus prepared: One or more, according to the number of fry, of Messrs. Peak, Frean and Co.'s "Town" biscuits, is crushed in a mortar to a moderately fine powder, and a lump of lean meat, about as large as a walnut, is allowed to each biscuit. The meat is thrown into the mortar, and being covered with biscuit-flour is pounded, being turned at intervals and re-covered with flour until a thin friable "meat biscuit" is produced; this is then fed out to the fish, small pieces being broken off and thrown lightly on to the water, when it will be shaken, worried, quarrelled over, and finally devoured.

These two are the best, safest, and most "growing" artificial foods that the fish-rearer can use; and no others will be recommended. If fry will not thrive well on them, they certainly will not on any other.

Whilst worms or gnats are used, that is for the first six or eight weeks after regular feeding is commenced, four meals a day are advised, or the worms may be suspended in a muslin bag under water, and then the fry always have food before them; but, if the stream be rapid, the worms work out through the muslin and roll along on the bottom, and are not caught by the fry, as they are apparently frightened by any object rolling in the water.

When the change of food takes place, three meals should be given at first, but as the fry grow stronger, and can take more at one feeding, the number may be diminished to two, given early in the morning and at, or a little before, sunset.   If, however, time permits, the midday meal should not be discontinued, as its effect on the growth of the fish is great, and prevents any tendency to "nibbling" or cannibalism.

As an extra, especially where they only get two regular feeds, carrion may be hung up over the stream or box if at some distance from a house, and the gentles falling therefrom will be greatly relished by the fry, when of a size to enable them to swallow a whole gentle.   This will as a rule be attained by the middle of June.

The fish-rearer must expect, however evenly-sized his fry may look at first, to find several go ahead of the rest, and rapidly to attain a size which makes them a terror to their smaller brethren, since they bully and even devour them. Such fish should be diligently sought for, and when caught, removed either to an open stream where they can shift for themselves, or to a separate box, where, being of equal size and strength, they will be less likely to damage one another. Otherwise sad havoc is sure to ensue.

The above system should be pursued, suiting the quantity and size of the food to that of the fish, as long as they are kept in an artificial state. This period may extend as long as the trout-rearer pleases : but, as a rule, space is at a premium for future use, and the fry are turned out as yearlings to shift for themselves in the open river in March or April of the year after that in which they were hatched. If, however, there be abundance of room, especially where they are in an open stream, it may be advisable to keep them in for two years, as

G

during the second year they put on flesh and growth to an extent which amply pays for the expense and trouble. Each person must, however, shape for himself the course to be pursued, as he alone can decide what will be the best to do under the circumstances.

If the general rules of procedure given above have been intelligently followed, disease will scarcely be observed, as that generally has its origin from foul water, overcrowding, and want or excess of proper food.

When disease does break out, however, it is a terrible scourge, as it spreads with fearful rapidity, and sweeps off the stock wholesale.

The best thing, perhaps, for the trout-rearer to do, should any such calamity occur, is to turn the fry out altogether into the open stream and let them go their own way, as instinct will doubtless guide them aright if left to follow out their own inclinations.

CHAPTER VII.

ENEMIES.

ALTHOUGH not connected with any of the actual processes of fish culture, the subject of the enemies of the eggs and fry of the salmonidæ is one of too great importance to the welfare of a fishery to be overlooked in this work. For, do what he may artificially, the breeder must, more or less, rely on the fecundity of the stream under his care. Besides this, the enemy will sometimes make a descent on the artificial preserves ; and, when once a footing has been established, will work havoc of the direst kind.

Enemies of the fish-eggs are legion. First come trout. They, following the actual parents, and tracing the nests by the arrangement of the gravel, root them up, and ruthlessly destroy the eggs of their predecessors, only anxious to secure progeny of their own.

We believe it would be wise, therefore, except where there is very ample room and accommodation for all the pairs of fishes to spawn on their own ground, and at their own time, to strip a number of females, even if the eggs are not wanted for artificial breeding. The males, too, might also be so treated, as, if there be a superfluity of them, the deaths through fighting are sure to be numerous. The under jaw of the male trout becomes hooked at spawning time, like that of the salmon, although not to the same extent; and fights of a very sanguinary character frequently take place. This plan need never be thought of where eggs are artificially hatched, as this system sufficiently depletes the occupants of the spawning ground; since those whose object has been obtained, quickly absent themselves, falling back down stream, to recruit their wasted condition.

All other fishes, too, are most greedy devourers of the ova of trout and salmon ; hence it is that the use of these eggs as bait is forbidden by law. In the Museum of Fish Culture, South Kensington, will be seen the cast of the stomach of a trout crammed with salmon eggs ; this is only one instance.

Besides piscine foes, the eggs and young fry have to contend against birds and beasts, which hunt them out and devour them to an untold extent ; water-fowl, rats, weasels, and many other creatures are enemies to be warned off the spawning ground.

About kingfishers there can be no doubt. These water-vultures will find out the whereabouts of young fish, especially young trout, from a long distance, and will not leave till the place has been cleared. Ornamental as the kingfisher, one of our handsomest British birds, is, he must be kept in check, or fish culture must be given up.

Having severely suffered from the visits of these birds, the writer ventures to caution the reader against any false security on this point. The bird may never be seen, but if the fish are wild and scurry about when approached, the odds are that the pest has been at work.

On one occasion a number of fry contained in a box were found to be very wild, and, on a search being made, a small hole in the wire netting was discovered, about two inches by one in size: as it was deemed impossible for a kingfisher to enter by it, no steps were taken till, on going to feed them one evening, an unusual sound was heard, and, on looking in, the creature was seen fluttering against the screen. Two sticks were procured, and the bird was eventually disabled, and killed by well-directed blows as it flew from end to end of the box. As a curiosity and a remarkably fine example it was entrusted to Mr. Edon, who has set it up with his usual care and skill.

Happily for pisciculture, Mr. Lane, trap-maker, of Wednesfield, has introduced some first-rate apparatus for their capture. His traps are small and circular, and are set on discs of wood, and supplied with a small perch, which, on the alighting of the bird, catches it by the feet. These discs of wood are put on small poles and set in sterams infested by the enemy.

Herons are dangerous to all sizes of fish, and should be kept under, especially at spawning time, when their prey resort to the shallows. A circle of traps, securely fastened to the ground, should be set round a heap of stones or mud, just rising above the surface of the water in spots frequented by these birds. They will settle on them when gorged, and be caught by the feet by the traps. Care should be taken in approaching a wounded heron, as the beak is very powerful and capable of inflicting a nasty wound.

Rats are a great nuisance in a stream, as they not only destroy eggs and very young fry, but also damage the banks and foul the bottom of the stream. Gins are very useful for them, when set in their runs, and a gun may be employed where its use is not calculated to disturb the game, if the stream runs through a preserve.

CHAPTER VIII.

STREAM CLEANING.

IT very often happens that a stream will have every element of suitability about it, but be so choked up by weeds and mud that, at first sight, it would be thought the last place to grow trout in. By dint, however, of the free use of mud-scoop and broom, it may, with hard work, be brought into order. The mud-scoop should be hemispherical, not merely a shovel, with a long handle, and the broom should be of whalebone. This material, though at first expensive, will answer in careful hands for a long time, and will give a "finish" to the bed of the stream which amply repays first cost. The scoop should be used as long as a fair amount is fetched out, then the broom is plied down stream to heap up the mud for the next removal; but, to finish off neatly, the broom should be worked over the ground again, down stream, the user drawing it towards him, so as to extinguish all footmarks and thoroughly cleanse the bed of the stréam. When once put in order, it should be kept in good condition, and should not be allowed again to become foul, as in this matter, as in so many others, " a stitch in time saves nine." Indeed, if there are three or four streams to be looked after, one man should be held responsible for their condition. A look over by him once or twice a week will ensure cleanliness, and save much labour. A moderate growth of water plants is to be allowed, but, especially in hot weather, these grow so rankly, that, unless kept in check, the result is that the "weeds" take possession of the place which should be occupied by the water.

CHAPTER IX.

CONCLUSION.

THIS little work has been written with the express object of so guiding the owner of water in the management of his fishery, that, by following out the broad principles laid down, disease may be averted, and success ensured. If personal acquaintance with all the practical details of breeding and rearing trout can give an authority to speak on such subjects, the writer may well claim that authority, as he has for some years carried on, with his own hands and under his own charge, a small fishery, the success of which has fairly astonished him. When first setting out he was so much hampered by doubts and fears, and perplexed about many things, that he hardly knew what course

to pursue; and right glad would he have been
to have had at hand such a book as this to refer
to. However, in any work on a subject which
is as yet in its infancy, many errors will neces-
sarily occur, and the writer hopes that those
herein will be found and corrected in a second
edition, should that be called for.

Before closing, the writer desires again to
thank Mr. Edon, Mr. Stone, and Mr. Green for
the information that they have from time to time
so readily furnished. To Mr. Frank Buckland
his acknowledgments are gratefully tendered;
as, by his energy and his hearty support and at
his instigation, the Museum of Fish Culture has
been established; for, though supported by
public money, it would never, in all probability,
have been established, had not Mr. Buckland
taken up the subject.

Some may very probably grumble at the
smallness of this book, and consider it super-
ficial, or think that the subject has not been

sufficiently elucidated. The answer to all such objections is that, when really understood, trout culture is intrinsically by no means a difficult matter, requiring years of study ; that its processes are all simple, requiring patience and practice, rather than genius in comprehension. And lastly, that to crowd a practical work with unnecessary matter, in other words to pad it out, is worse than useless, as the fewer words that are used the more easily are they retained in the memory.

LONDON : PRINTED BY WILLIAM CLOWES AND SONS, STAMFORD STREET
AND CHARING CROSS.